Original title:
Moss in the Morning

Copyright © 2025 Creative Arts Management OÜ
All rights reserved.

Author: Giselle Montgomery
ISBN HARDBACK: 978-1-80567-298-2
ISBN PAPERBACK: 978-1-80567-597-6

Camouflage of the Early Hours

In slippers soft, I tread so slow,
The garden greets with a leafy glow.
My coffee spills, a morning blight,
It blends with greens, oh what a sight!

The squirrels laugh from branches high,
As I trip over the roots nearby.
They toss their acorns, a game, it seems,
While I chase shadows and sip my dreams.

Mysteries in the Sylvan Depths

A face peeks out from the frayed ground,
A frog, or perhaps a foe I found.
It croaks a tune, a morning song,
As if to say, 'You've been here long!'

The ants parade in their tiny suits,
While I lost my shoes among the roots.
They march on by without a care,
Unfazed by humans with morning hair.

The Celestial Charm of Green

The dew drops gather, a sparkling spree,
As I dance poorly, just me and the bee.
They buzz around with a waggle and twist,
I'm the clumsy human, a morning mist!

The grass tickles toes, a funny delight,
But watch where you sit, it may just bite!
With squirming worms as my jolly crew,
Nature chuckles; what's a girl to do?

Footprints on Nature's Lush Carpet

With every step, I leave my mark,
Among the ferns, a playful lark.
The earth, soft, like a giant bed,
Invites my slip, oh what a spread!

My footprints squish in a silly way,
As I frolic through the morning play.
And giggles echo, the trees agree,
For mornings here should be wild and free.

Soft Breath in the Underbrush

In the hush of dawn's embrace,
Squeaky leaves hide their grace.
A critter snickers, quick as a dart,
With morning breath, it's a smelly start.

Frogs croak jokes, quite obscene,
As slugs slide in their slick sheen.
A playful breeze pulls on a twig,
Nature giggles, not quite big.

Textures of the Dawn's Cloak

Patches soft, like grandma's quilt,
Underfoot, where dreams are built.
A rabbit trips on its own two feet,
Laughing moss, what a silly treat!

Sunbeams tickle the leaves with glee,
Fungi grins in pure jubilee.
A wobbly snail competes for pace,
As the sun paints smiles on every face.

Glade Beneath a Gentle Sun

Squirrels dance in a nutty spree,
While shadows play hide and seek with me.
A friendly worm hops up to jest,
With squishy jokes, it's truly blessed!

The ground thrives in a comedic fight,
As ladybugs take off in flight.
Each blossom winks, a floral flair,
Saying, "Join us, if you dare!"

The Symbiosis of Daybreak

Morning giggles weave through the air,
Nature's pranksters, everywhere!
A beetle's hat flips in the breeze,
As grass blades knit their silly tease.

Dew drops scatter like tiny cheers,
As sunlight tickles my sleepy ears.
A chubby toad croaks out a tune,
Quite the entertainers, morning's boon!

Dew-Kissed Serenity

A tiny world where raindrops play,
On grassy hills, they dance and sway.
The sun peeks in with a sleepy grin,
While ants parade in their morning spin.

A ladybug dons her emerald hat,
Chasing shadows, oh where's she at?
With giggles from the flowers so bright,
They tickle blades till they giggle light.

The Lush Embrace of Dawn

Beneath the tree, a squirrel lies low,
Dreaming of nuts, all in a row.
He stirs and flips, thinks he might fly,
But lands on his tail — oh my, oh my!

The wily fox with a twinkle in eyes,
Stalks the morning snacks, oh what a surprise!
With a hop and a skip, he tries to sneak,
But trips on a twig — now that's quite meek!

Verdant Shadows Gather

The ferns waggle as breezes tease,
While critters frolic with ease,
A toad sings loud, just for a laugh,
As clovers giggle in grassy half.

A butterfly trips on its colorful wing,
While a peacock struts, thinking it's the king.
They collide in a tumble of funny flair,
Spreading joy in the cool morning air.

Soft Earth's Gentle Caress

Underfoot, the blanket feels like a hug,
Where worms wriggle, nice and snug.
The beetles march as if on parade,
While mushrooms chuckle, all mislaid.

In puddles, reflections dance with glee,
As frogs lead the choir in a symphony.
With every ribbit, a tune so silly,
Morning's bounty brings joy, oh so frilly!

Echoes in the Soft Underbrush

In the woods a squirrel pranced,
Whiskers twitching, quite entranced.
A giggly frog began to croak,
'Is that a dance or just a joke?'

Beneath the ferns, a snail did slide,
Wearing on its shell a pride.
With every bounce, the leaves they shush,
While rowdy ants form quite the rush.

A Tangle of Green Lives

A rabbit tripped on tangled grass,
Hopped like it had quite the sass.
A worm popped up, said 'What's the fuss?'
'Can't you see? We're all in a bus!'

Then came a bee with a fuzzy hat,
Said, 'I'm late, where's the party at?'
They chuckled loud, a merry throng,
In nature's tune, they danced along.

Golden Glimmers of a New Day

The sun peeks in, a playful tease,
Painting shadows with such ease.
A ladybug with spots so bright,
Practices its pirouette in flight.

A lizard lounges on a stone,
Claiming it as its own throne.
With every beam, it tries to grin,
Saying, 'Look at me, where have you been?'

Under the Weight of Dew

A spider webs its art on grass,
Impressed, a snail stops to amass.
'What are you doing, all grand and bright?'
'Just catching bugs in morning light!'

The droplets shimmer like tiny stars,
And caterpillars dream of cars.
With laughter echoing through the glen,
The day begins, and it joins in again.

Radiance in Hidden Hollows

In secret spots where shadows play,
A carpet green begins the day.
It wears a coat of glistening dew,
A dance of laughs in vibrant hue.

The tiny critters have their say,
In nature's chat, they twist and sway.
A frog, a snail, and bugs in line,
They share their jokes, they sip on brine.

A Tapestry of Tiny Worlds

Upon the ground, a quilt of cheer,
Where tiny things find refuge here.
A ladybug with spots of red,
Is ruling realms from where it's fed.

A bustling ant joins in the fun,
Its little legs go on the run.
While spiders spin their silken threads,
Creating tales in leafy beds.

The Gentle Touch of First Light

The sun peeks through with playful charm,
As creatures stretch with light's warm balm.
A setup stage where all belong,
In nature's concert, they sing wrong.

A rabbit hops to join the beat,
It tumbles down, oh such a feat!
The woodpecker, with rhythm strong,
Admits its tap was just too long.

Mysteries Beneath the Trees

Under leafy giants, secrets hide,
Where giggles of the forest bide.
A squirrel tells a tall, tall tale,
Of nuts that danced and kicked, not frail.

With shadows flicking, giggles rise,
As creatures plot their small surprise.
The clever roots, they twist and twine,
A caper where the toads align.

Treading on Nature's Velvet

With fluffy greens beneath my toes,
I skip and dance, I strike a pose.
Each step a squish, a silly plop,
Who knew that muddy bliss won't stop?

I faceplant down, my friends all laugh,
I've become a nature's photograph.
The ground, it giggles, oh so sly,
As I get up, I can't deny!

A tuft of fluff stuck in my hair,
I prance about without a care.
A slip, a trip, more laughter sounds,
I'm nature's jester, crowned in grounds!

So if you tread on velvet green,
Expect to join this giggle scene.
With every step, just let it flow,
Nature's humor, steal the show!

Secrets of the Shaded Hollow

In shadows deep where whispers play,
I found a frog who had to say,
'Why hop alone like some dull chap?
Join our party, take a nap!'

With mushrooms sprouting like a throne,
The crickets chirp a secret tone.
A squirrel tossed acorns like confetti,
While beetles danced, all looking petty.

'Your shoes are noisy!' one bug said,
'Just listen to the things we've bred.'
So I wiggled my toes, all shy,
They laughed and said, 'Oh my, oh my!'

With each new secret that I learned,
The shade became my world, I turned.
I twirled and jumped in pure delight,
In this hollow, everything's just right!

Cradled by Earth's Silence

In a damp nook where the sun won't peek,
I stumbled on a snail so chic.
'I'm fabulous!' he said with pride,
'Come have a seat, please try my ride.'

We cruised on leaves, in slippery bliss,
Around the pond, a slimy kiss.
The lily pads clapped, what a sight,
As frogs croaked tunes, all day and night!

A worm popped up, 'Join our parade!'
'The grand spectacle, I've just made!'
They jiggled and wiggled in harmony,
While I laughed, feeling so free!

Cradled here, I felt so spry,
With slimy pals, under the sky.
In the quiet, I found my song,
With nature's crew, where all belong!

The Breath of Velvet Flora

Oh plants galore in vibrant hues,
They sway and dance, like they're bemused.
'Join us!', they whisper, 'Don't be shy,'
But watch your feet, the ground's awry!

A tulip told me, 'You're quite a tease,
With those big shoes, you're sure to squeeze!'
I burst out laughing, they all chimed in,
'Come join the troupe, let the fun begin!'

With petals flapping all around,
I stumbled, lost, upon soft ground.
'Come nibble here!' a daisy cried,
I took a bite, then ran to hide!

In this lush realm, I found my flair,
The flora's laughter filled the air.
With every giggle, every sway,
I tumbled in bloom, brightening the day!

Velvet Carpet Beneath Footfalls

A squishy surprise beneath my shoes,
Nature's prank, in morning's hues.
I tiptoe softly, a giggle slips,
As nature tickles my clumsy trips.

The forest floor, a soft embrace,
I wonder if it likes this race.
With every step, a little crunch,
A breakfast dance of a silly lunch.

Little critters peek and stare,
They're shocked to see me, unaware.
I trip on roots, they cheer with glee,
This comedy show is just for me.

But as I stroll, the sun breaks through,
The carpet sparkles with dew's fresh hue.
In a world where laughter takes the stage,
I leave my footprints, the forest's page.

Dawn's Breath on Forest Floors

The morning breeze, a gentle tease,
Whispers of laughter rustle the trees.
I dance along, all spry and free,
But stumble over my own two feet.

A chorus of chirps, nature's jokes,
They giggle at me, these forest folks.
I wave my arms, a grand charade,
Fallen branches become my aide.

In this lively space, I'm the star,
With twigs for props, oh how bizarre!
Each step is a punchline, oh what a sight,
As shadows stretch and chase the light.

The sun rises high, laughter ensues,
Nature's comedy, all for my muse.
With every giggle these woods enjoy,
I skip along, nature's silly boy.

Nature's Quiet Awakening

In the stillness, the giggles rise,
Nature wakes with playful sighs.
A frog croaks out a sleepy song,
While crickets laugh, all night long.

The leaves chuckle in a morning breeze,
As I hop along with wobbly knees.
Each footprint leaves a ticklish trace,
The ground erupts in nature's face.

As squirrels scamper with little darts,
They think it's funny—who steals hearts?
With each scamper, they slide on by,
The forest floor, their slip-and-slide.

In this awakening, laughter thrives,
Nature's humor, the best of lives.
I join the cheer, a silly blend,
Every step is where joy transcends.

Moonlight's Remnants at First Light

The moon fades out with a big 'Ta-da!'
As sunlight spills like warm sarsaparilla.
I watch as shadows begin to flee,
With a wink between the trunks and me.

The night's tales whisper secrets low,
While the first rays scamper to and fro.
I trip over roots that stick like glue,
And laugh as fireflies bid adieu.

The giggles linger on dew-kissed leaves,
Nature's stand-up, oh how it weaves.
I settle in for a show of glee,
As dawn's light pranks are all for me.

With each small skip, my joy in tow,
I'm the audience for nature's show.
As the forest chuckles, I can't resist,
At moonlight's end, oh what a twist!

A Dance of Green Shadows

In the break of day, they wiggle and sway,
Tiny greens with a secret ballet.
Twisting and turning, what do they see?
Do they giggle at humans, just like me?

Beneath the old tree, they gather for fun,
Underneath the sunlight, out of the run.
They whisper and chuckle, not caring to hide,
While I trip on twigs, trying to glide.

A party of stickers, a flora brigade,
They twirl and they leap in the sunshine parade.
I laugh at their antics, what a quirky sight,
Green wiggly dancers, a true morning delight!

With sandals, I venture, a slip and a slide,
Yet they don't seem worried, they giggle with pride.
Caught in their carpet, what a silly trap,
They dance on my shoes, oh what a mishap!

The Hidden Life of Unseen Ferns

Under the ferns, a drama unfolds,
Silent and sneaky, the laughter it holds.
With a wink and a nod, they keep things discreet,
Pretending to nap, with feathers and greet.

While I'm out searching for lost morning socks,
They're curling up secrets behind woody blocks.
Each crinkle and rustle, a chuckle I hear,
As they plot their next prank with nothing to fear.

Their bright green attire, pure fashion divine,
Camas and dreams, they swirl in a line.
With a shy little wave, they wave me along,
Inviting my laughter to join in their song.

Yet step on a twig and the whole house will know,
Their giggles erupt like an oil-slicked show.
So I watch from a distance, I try to refrain,
But burst into giggles, and it's all in vain!

Nature's Morning Embrace

In the cradle of dawn, all things come alive,
A snuggly green blanket, where silliness thrives.
With a sprout here and there, a warm fuzzy hug,
They bask in the glow, not needing a rug.

Photogenic critters have come out to play,
Bouncing and tumbling in a leafy ballet.
While I sip my coffee, they dance on the dew,
Creating a ruckus that's goofy but true.

Giggling gigabytes, they jiggle and shake,
A quirky parade that I just can't fake.
With a simple salute, they nod and they cheer,
To the tunes of the morning, oh so very clear!

So if you feel heavy or lost in your day,
Just seek out the greens, let your worries all sway.
Lifted by laughter, under bright sunbeams,
Nature's embrace is just full of sweet dreams!

Cradled in Softness

Soft as a whisper, they cushion the ground,
In a world of green fluff, all silliness found.
Underfoot miracles, a jittery crew,
Each step that I take, they giggle anew.

Down by the stream, where the gigglers reside,
They giggle and shimmer, no reason to hide.
Dancing in puddles, with no care at all,
As they join for a splash in a silly free-for-all!

A tickle of laughter, a bounce in the breeze,
They sway with the rhythm, oh what a tease!
In tangled up threads, their joy can be felt,
Bouncing in circles, as if laughing at belt.

Rooted in humor, they brighten my way,
Each step is a jest, come join the display.
So here I am treading, on this plush green stage,
Sharing in laughter, let's turn a new page!

Beneath the Canopy's Invitation

Under the trees' wild embrace,
Frogs in tuxedos leap with grace.
Squirrels with acorns, plotting a heist,
Dance like they're at a wild feast!

Sunlight tickles the forest floor,
A raccoon rolls by, what a bore!
He thinks he's a bandit, sly and spry,
In search of snacks, oh my, oh my!

Birds hold a concert, off-key and loud,
Owls rolling eyes, they won't be proud.
With laughter hidden in every leaf,
Nature's own comic, beyond belief!

So come join the fun, it's quite a show,
Beneath the canopy where antics flow.
The trees whisper secrets, giggles they share,
In this playful realm, without a care!

The Spirit of Green Awakens

A patch of green starts to giggle,
As worms get ready to dance and wriggle.
The ants are marching, proud and spry,
In their little suits, oh my, oh my!

In the early hours, a rabbit sneers,
"Catch me if you can!"—then disappears.
A beetle's strutting, feeling quite grand,
Waving to friends, oh isn't life just planned!

Sunbeams are slapping the dew like fun,
Each droplet glistens, a race has begun.
With leaves as umbrellas, laughter's the tune,
The spirit joyously greets the afternoon!

So next time you wander, take a glance,
At those cheeky critters daring to prance.
For in every crack, and nook you find,
The spirit's awake, unconfined!

Emerald Threads of Light

Threads of green twist and twine,
A patchwork quilt by design.
Caterpillars play tag, so sly,
Chasing each other, oh my, oh my!

Sun rays sneak through, tickling each spore,
Mushrooms gossip behind the door.
The shadows chuckle, hiding in strife,
As ferns wave hello—a laugh at life!

In this realm where silliness thrives,
Every twig teems with tiny lives.
A snail in sunglasses takes quite the stroll,
With dreams of glory, that's his goal!

Beneath this canopy, laughter unfolds,
The stories of green turn playful and bold.
So join the parade of whimsical sight,
In emerald threads, with sheer delight!

A Tapestry of Life Unfurled

Life weaves a fabric, vibrant and bright,
With threads of humor in morning light.
A porcupine prances, forgetting his spikes,
While turtles race, oh are they like bikes!

The dandelions dance, puffing their cheeks,
"Look at us blow!" is what nature speaks.
While bees in a buzz sing off-key tunes,
For silly critters, the world is their boon!

The creek giggles, splashing about,
In puddles of joy, it has no doubt.
With chipmunks juggling acorns on stage,
They invite you all, come join the page!

So remember the tapestry, wild and free,
In each tiny laugh, there's a jubilee.
For nature is funny, and so is the day,
With quips and quirks just a giggle away!

Dawn's Silken Embrace

The sun peeked in with a grin,
Bouncing light off the dampened skin.
Frogs croaked tunes in a jovial spree,
While ants formed bands as if it were free.

Dewdrop dancers on blades so slick,
Wobbling round like they learned a trick.
They giggle and shimmer, a lumpy parade,
While squirrels make nests with the leaves they invade.

A sleepy snail took a sprightly leap,
Over a rock, oh what a heap!
He slipped and slid, a clumsy delight,
While shadows play in the soft morning light.

Breezes flirt with the petals shy,
As flowers giggle at the clouds that sigh.
Dawn's giggles ripple through each leafy vein,
In this morning revel, we're free from all pain.

Life Awaits in Quietude.

In the stillness, odd noises creep,
A chirp, a gurgle, almost a peep.
A hedgehog rolls in an unlikely role,
Dreaming of snacks, not a worry in the soul.

The teapot cackles, a kettle in tow,
While squirrels play chess, don't you know?
With acorns as pieces, they hash out the game,
Not caring a wit for fortune or fame.

A bendy worm launches a twisty dive,
In moist terrain, oh how they thrive!
While sleepy bumblebees buzz like mad,
Chasing the drips, oh what a fad!

Here life awaits, with its quirks on parade,
For every shady spot is perfectly made.
Laughter erupts in a curious show,
As nature's comic waits for her bow.

Emerald Veil of Dawn

Green blankets spread across the field,
With laughter sprouting where dreams are healed.
A butterfly wiggles with style so grand,
Practicing twirls on an invisible strand.

A raccoon with flair, painted eyes in glee,
Steals breakfast crumbs, as bold as can be.
His jester cap flops in the early light,
As worms complain, oh what a fright!

Crickets chime in with a ribbit and chirp,
Composing a symphony with each little burp.
The daisies sway, they know the score,
While the dandelions laugh as they roll on the floor.

Life's quirky vibe in shades of green,
Morning mischief in every scene.
With chuckles and grins, the day takes flight,
In this emerald veil, everything feels right.

Whispering Green Awakenings

Rustling leaves tell tales so bold,
Of sleepy critters and stories untold.
A line of ants holds a morning chat,
While an old tortoise sports a sunhat.

The daffodils gossip, their stories obscure,
Of how each petal, soft and pure,
Hopes for a sprinkle, a drop, or a sigh,
To dance with the breezes that flutter by.

Frogs wear spectacles, they read the news,
While snacking on flies, they cannot refuse.
As shadows play tag with the morning glow,
The world wakes up, oh what a show!

Sunshine nudges the slumbering ground,
With tickles of warmth that spin all around.
In giggles of green, daybreak reborn,
Every little creature greets the morn.

Awakening to Life in Quiet Places

In the dawn's cool embrace, it unfolds,
Little worlds awakening, stories untold.
A critter sneezes, it's a raucous affair,
As sunlight tickles the air, unaware.

Beneath every leaf, secrets giggle and dance,
The squirrels perform their acrobatic prance.
A frog croaks a tune, with dubious flair,
While butterflies wonder, 'Is it time for a dare?'

A snail takes a stroll, oh, what a parade,
As shadows of trees join in the charade.
With each tiny step, the Earth starts to hum,
In these quiet spots, how can we not succumb?

They're breeding grounds for laughs, and titters galore,
Where every trivial moment opens a door.
To giggles and chuckles, let's cherish the sight,
In places like this, the morning feels right.

Verdant Echoes of New Beginnings

Sprouts burst forth, in a giggly spree,
With leaves that whisper, 'Come dance with me!'
Nature's a jester, in green and in gold,
While dandelions plot mischief, bold.

A floppy-eared rabbit, on an old wooden throne,
Holds court for the critters, all gathered, well-known.
He cracks up the crowd with a carrot-based joke,
Leaves rustle in laughter, wakes up the oak.

The bugs are consultants in regal attire,
Arguing fiercely on who needs more fire.
They serve up their wisdom, with giggles and grins,
In the theatre of growth, everyone wins!

So, let's toast the sprouts, in their jubilant run,
Cheers to their laughter, from morning till sun.
In this yard of laughter, the world seems to sing,
Amid echoes of joy, new beginnings take wing.

Hues of Dawn in the Thicket

As dawn's first blush spills through leafy screens,
A squirrel wears pants made of silly green seams.
He struts with a flair, in a riot of style,
Nature's own runway, bringing giggles worthwhile.

The sun starts to tickle the sleepy old trees,
Causing branches to chuckle, like a light summer breeze.
A woodpecker knocks out a catchy new song,
While the owls in pajamas just nod along strong.

In this woodland ruckus, where laughter abounds,
The tiniest critters are best with the sounds.
Ants in a conga, they party in ranks,
Making paths that are funny, and full of odd pranks.

With colors so vivid, they dance and they sway,
How joyously bright is this mischief-filled day!
Among shades of sunrise, let giggles awake,
In the thicket of life, there's much fun to make.

The Tenderness of Nature's Blanket

A soft quilt of green wraps the ground so tight,
   Inviting each creature to bask in the light.
A frolicsome worm, in a dance with pure glee,
   Wiggles and jiggles, 'Oh come look at me!'

The daisies are gossiping, all white and aloof,
'What's up with the daisies? Let's spill the goof!'
   With petals a-flutter and giggles in tow,
   They share all their secrets, in a fluttery flow.

The raindrops bring laughter as they plop and they splat,
   Making puddles where frogs throw a splashy old spat.
   While butterflies sip on a dew-dripped surprise,
   They snicker and dart, like they're wearing disguise.

So here's to the moments while nature's awake,
   Where each gentle whisper makes ripples and shakes.
      In this tender embrace, let hilarity bloom,
   As the beauty unfolds, we'll dance in the room.

Ferns and Dreams Beneath the Sun

Ferns wave cheerily, a dance so bold,
They giggle together, their secrets untold.
Sunbeams tickle, both shy and bright,
While shadows play games, a merry sight.

A ladybug strolls, dressed up just right,
As grass blades gossip with all their might.
Insects are busy, with jobs quite absurd,
A choir of chirps, and none have a word.

A snail takes a selfie, all slimy and slow,
The butterfly winks with a colorful show.
Fluffy the cloud drifts, a fluffball of cheer,
Whispers of wind reach each ear with a jeer.

Each morning's a circus, a farcical tease,
Nature's oddball cast performing with ease.
Laughter erupts as the sun gives a grin,
In this green-gold world, let the fun begin!

The Earth's Kind Embrace

Under thick blankets of spongy delight,
The earth's gentle hug, it feels just right.
Squirrels debate over acorns at play,
While worms wiggle through, in their own cabaret.

The trees join the feasting, with branches that sway,
Wishing for snacks they can nibble all day.
Hats made of leaves on a headless old stump,
Will it dance with the breeze, or just be a lump?

Ants march like soldiers, all ready for fame,
As they charge through the dew, what a silly game!
Their tiny parade makes the tiniest news,
While blossoms all giggle, a party to use.

So if you get lost in this wild, leafy land,
Just follow the chuckles, a guide that's quite grand.
For laughter and joy in this earth's sweet embrace,
Make every day's dawn a whimsical race!

Echoes of the Morning Blush

Sunrise winks softly, a cheeky old friend,
While shadows play hopscotch, with no need to blend.
A power nap taken by daisies in streams,
As the world wakes up, still caught in its dreams.

Clouds puff their chests, like they own the whole sky,
While rain drops like marbles fall down from the high.
Petunias gossip, their petals a-flutter,
Whispering secrets as soft as ripe butter.

The sun yawns aloud, spreading laughter and cheer,
As bad jokes are told by the breeze whispering near.
A squirrel in striped socks does a jig by the tree,
While flowers all burst into raucous glee.

Every morning's blush, an echo of fun,
With tiny green critters all out for a run.
In this realm of giggles, where mornings are pure,
Let's dance with the dawn, our joys to procure!

A Symphony of Green and Gold

Nature's orchestra tunes with a chuckle and cheer,
As crickets warm up, the beat's drawing near.
A rabbit in rhythm, with hops all around,
And buzzing bees humming a sweet, silly sound.

Tall grasses sway, auditioning their bends,
While daisies sway sweetly, making new friends.
The sun plays the flute, with rays shining bold,
And the sky's painted laughter in brilliant gold.

Each leaf has a part in this playful refrain,
As the brook sings along, its voice pure and sane.
Frogs croak their solos, a croon and a croak,
Creating a symphony, laughter awoke.

In this jolly concert, let all join the fun,
With green and gold patches basking in sun.
A morning so lively, let your spirit take flight,
In nature's grand symphony, everything feels right!

Secrets of the Green Canopy

In shadows deep where whispers play,
A squirrel's dance steals light of day.
The leaves giggle in gentle breeze,
While snails hold meetings with great ease.

The fungi wear their little hats,
And gossip flies among the rats.
Each branch is full of quiet tricks,
As nature plays its silly flicks.

Bright-eyed frogs in tuxedos hop,
Discussing bugs and bugging stops.
A winking owl, smart and sly,
Wants toast with jam, oh my, oh my!

The forest has a joke or two,
Its jokes are green, its laughter true.
The hidden paths of soft delight,
Lead to a giggle every night.

Emerald Dreams Under Pale Sun

A beetle rolls a tiny ball,
While daisies laugh and giggle tall.
The sun peeks shy, unsure of play,
It tickles grass in a merry way.

Bunny tails fluff like fairy dust,
As flowers sway, it's quite a must.
The groundhog yawns, then trips on dew,
"Oh dear," he laughs, "I'm stuck like glue!"

The ants parade in perfect rows,
With crumbs of cake from nearby foes.
They toast their feast and sing a tune,
A cupcake dream beneath the moon.

A plucky worm spins tales of glee,
With secrets whispered to the tree.
In emerald realms of giggling fun,
The day is bright, the smiles are spun.

The Calm Before the Awakening

The birds decide it's time to shriek,
As sleepy bugs play hide and seek.
A cat pretends to take a nap,
But dreams of chases make her clap.

The coffee beans do wiggle and jive,
While morning glories start to thrive.
The sun's a prankster, peeks then hides,
While sleepy plants are on joy rides.

The breeze brings whispers of the day,
Where mischief rules in playtime's sway.
A squirrel's stole a peanut prize,
Excuse me while I roll my eyes.

Awake, awake, the crickets cry,
With laugh tracks hidden in the sky.
The calm that flirts with silly cheer,
Can turn a frown into a sneer.

Lush Tones at Daybreak

In the shortly hours, laughter wakes,
A slug complains of crunchy flakes.
The trees hum tunes of green delight,
While shadows play in morning light.

A froggy band croaks out a tune,
Conducted by a fancy moon.
The daisies sway; they twirl and spin,
While butterflies join in with a grin.

The wise old owl cracks silly jokes,
As drowsy flowers start their pokes.
The pebbles chuckle at the dew,
Who knew they'd spark a tear or two?

The morning whispers soft and clear,
With every creature lending cheer.
In lush tones where the funny flows,
Nature's giggle ever grows!

Emerald Lullabies

In the hush of dawn's embrace,
A carpet greets your sleepy face.
It tickles toes and makes you laugh,
A gentle prank from nature's path.

Shh, dear friend, don't make a fuss,
You're stuck beneath the greenish crust.
A soft caress, the earth's delight,
Whispers, "Sleep in shades of light."

Frogs croak jokes while peeking out,
As morning's blush seduces doubt.
It's nature's wink, a whimsical spree,
Where every blade becomes a tease.

And should you trip on squidgy ground,
Remember prancing makes the sound.
So giggle freely with no care,
Embrace the green - it's everywhere!

Surrender to the Soft Earth

Close your eyes; feel that plush thrill,
Underfoot, the squish is real.
A palace made of verdancy,
Where even snails sip tea with glee.

The surface bounces with a grin,
As critters wiggle and spin.
Slipping on a hearty patch,
Your shoes scream, 'Oh, what a catch!'

A family of ants in a parade,
Marching loudly on their escapade.
While dew drops giggle on their way,
Chasing the sun, 'Just let us play!'

Embrace the tickle, revel in fun,
The world's a joke when it's just begun.
So yield to earth's fuzzy embrace,
Where laughter dances, and cheer takes place.

Veils of Nature's Slumber

Under a blanket of emerald plush,
The laughter of critters, oh such a rush!
Morning snoozers wake with a yawn,
As flowers stretch and stretch at dawn.

Grass blades form a ticklish dance,
As squirrels perform their acrobat's prance.
With every step, a tiny prank,
Their mischief hidden in the flank.

Entities of soft and squishy mayhem,
Compose a symphony of whimsy and mayhem.
Roll in the green, with squeals and delight,
Each squishy inch, a joyous sight.

But be warned; the damp may stick,
As laughter loud can leave you slick.
So wade with giggles, embrace the sweep,
For nature's layers are yours to keep!

Awakening the Verdant Veil

As dawn peeks through the leafy dome,
The green world wakes to call you home.
A whisper here, a chuckle there,
Nature's plush carpet, with mischief to share.

You'll find wet shoes and joyous slips,
A dance with nature, in playful dips.
Every stone hides a cheeky grin,
Soft earth beckons, "Come on in!"

The world's so green, it's hard to tread,
As giggles bubble in your head.
So jump and splash, let the fun explode,
In this vivid realm, let laughter corrode.

With every squish, a playful shout,
As laughter rings through the leafy route.
Awake to joy, let spirits sail,
In this bright land, where giggles prevail!

Cradled in Nature's Parlor

In a cozy green chair, the bugs find their snacks,
Frogs sing the tune while the snail makes its tracks.
A squirrel tells jokes, with acorns for props,
While the ladybug giggles, and the fun never stops.

The flowers all wink, in their colorful dress,
Making fun of the weeds, that always digress.
"What's your favorite game?" asks the bumblebee,
"Hide and seek, of course, but you can't find me!"

Teacups of dew sit on leaf-tipped tables,
With ants in their tuxes, discussing their fables.
The breeze tells a tale, and the branches all sway,
As laughter erupts in nature's cabaret.

At dusk they all gather, to share a good cheer,
But a raccoon steals snacks, oh dear, oh dear!
Yet they all just chuckle, it's a riotous sight,
In nature's own parlor, where everything's right.

Sunlight's Dance on Tender Leaves

Sunlight tumbles, giggles bright,
As shadows play tag in morning light.
A leaf slips and slides, in a playful race,
While a dragonfly zips, with a grin on its face.

The daisies hold hands, in a field of delight,
While daisies debate if they're white or just slight.
A breeze whispers secrets, the trees start to sway,
As the tulips all cheer, for the colorful play!

Near the pond, ducks quack, doing pirouettes,
While frogs in tuxedos send out their regrets.
"Did we miss the party?" they croak in dismay,
While the fish dive below, in their own kind of ballet.

And as day rolls onward, with laughter and cheer,
They whisper of stories, for all who will hear.
In this sunny ballet, where joy seems to please,
Every creature is twirling, oh what a tease!

Beneath the Hushed Canopy

In shadows so cozy, where whispers abound,
A chipmunk finds treasures that he can't quite pound.
He stocks up his pantry, with berries in line,
While the wise old owl hoots, "Hey, this plan's divine!"

The leaves overhead gossip, of squirrels that play,
Who think they can leap from one branch to sway.
But mid-air they freeze, surprised by a gust,
And land with a thud, in the pile of soft dust.

A raccoon runs past, with a half-eaten pear,
While the fireflies twinkle like jewels in the air.
They flash a bright hello, with giggles they glide,
A midnight parade where the critters all hide.

The rustles keep growing, it's a party of sorts,
Old badgers in bowties offer snacks and retorts.
In this leafy retreat, full of giggles and fun,
Every critter knows that the night has begun!

Oasis at First Light

Where sunlight spills joy, on the dew-laden grass,
Each critter awakens, as night fades to pass.
A hedgehog spins tales, of dreams from the dark,
While turtles debate if they'll race to the park.

A clamorous chorus of birds starts to chirp,
As foxes in sneakers prepare for a slurp.
The river rolls by, with a snicker and swirl,
And the frog jumps in, for a delightful twirl.

Monkeys swing in, with a playful delight,
Sharing banana jokes, oh what a sight!
The sun casts its rays, with friendly designs,
While the bees find their dance in perfect sunshine lines.

As days meet the dawn, with laughter so bright,
Every creature rejoices in this morning light.
In this radiant haven, where silliness thrives,
Nature laughs together, oh what pranks it devises!

Whispers of Dewy Greens

Dewdrops giggle on leaves, in a dance,
Caught in a breeze, they seem to prance.
A worm tells a joke, quite a delight,
As ants make a march, in morning light.

Gophers peek out, wearing their hats,
Startled by frogs in their morning spats.
Twirling around in a leafy parade,
Nature's own circus, never a charade.

Bugs buzzing in tune, a laugh out loud,
Singing to flowers, all bright and proud.
With every squish of grass beneath feet,
The dance floor awaits on this mini street.

A snail slips and slides, oh what a show,
A slowest of races, but whispers do flow.
With each droplet's sparkle, life feels so fine,
In the realm of the green, where all things entwine.

Beneath the Canopy's Breath

Under the branches, the squirrels conspire,
To steal all the snacks, they work like a choir.
With tiny paws, they plot and they scheme,
While the rabbits just giggle, living the dream.

A chubby hedgehog rolls, taking a spin,
Dressed in spiky charm, oh where to begin?
The sunlight peeks down, tickling their toes,
In the world of the wild, anything goes!

Chattering birds in a raucous trio,
Trading sweet secrets, oh what a video!
A rabbit stumbles, steals a quick glance,
While the frogs chuckle in their morning dance.

With laughter exchanged under clouds so bright,
The capers unfold in the warm morning light.
In nature's big show, they play without strife,
Creating such chaos, it's the best kind of life!

Lush Carpet at Daybreak

The ground sprawls out in a vibrant hue,
A soft, squishy mass where fairies brew.
They trip on their wings, the silly sprites,
Dancing on grass in their pajama flights.

With hues of green, they paint the day,
Flipping and flopping in their own ballet.
A beetle claps hands, joining the fray,
Declaring the start of his serious play!

Ladybugs lounge, quite the sunbathers,
While bumblebees buzz like relentless haters.
Each whisper of wind makes a ruckus anew,
As nature, it seems, loves a good view.

Beneath the tall oaks, the game has begun,
With laughter and joy, they all have some fun.
The lush carpet welcomes each creature's charm,
In this green expanse, there's never a harm!

Shadows of a Glistening Dawn

In the early light, shadows stretch long,
The critters awake, join in the song.
A raccoon in shades, he's quite the cool bloke,
Wears mismatched socks, and loves a good joke.

With sunlight giggling upon the ground,
All the little creatures spin round and round.
The spiders weave tales in delicate threads,
While the chipmunks laugh, filling their heads.

A froggy conspiracy with plans so grand,
He hops to his buddy, the best-laid band.
With splashes and splatters, they jump with glee,
Creating such chaos, pure jubilee!

The day waves hello from its bright debut,
While the world teems with laughter, fresh as the dew.
In the embrace of light, the mischief they flaunt,
Makes morning more playful, it's quite the jaunt!

Nature's Morning Call

A damp surprise beneath my shoe,
A squishy mess, oh what a view!
It giggles softly, what a joke,
Nature's carpet, a soggy cloak.

A little frog jumps with a splash,
Who knew mornings could be such a clash?
Waking up with a jump and a yelp,
Nature's alarm with no chance to help!

The trees are laughing, the breeze gives a tease,
As I trip over roots, such a breeze!
My coffee spills, it's quite absurd,
Start the day — who's really disturbed?

Yet here I stand, in earth's embrace,
With mud on my shoes, and a smile on my face.
So bring on the chuckles and the glee,
Nature's morning antics are fun for me!

Secrets Veiled in Greenery

Beneath the leaves where shadows play,
A critter peeks to start the day.
Is that a squirrel or just a prank?
Nature's theater — full of shank!

Fungi popping like a birthday treat,
They celebrate on my morning street.
With colors bright and shapes so wild,
I laugh out loud, I'm such a child!

A snail in slippers, what a sight!
How slow can one be before it's night?
He wiggles forth without a care,
In this secret world, I stop and stare.

So let the whispers keep their jest,
In emerald cloaks, we are all guests.
A morning giggle, so full of cheer,
In nature's game, there's nothing to fear!

Soft Green Mornings Unfurl

In the chill of dawn, things creep,
A frog in slippers, oh so deep.
He leaps from leaf to leaf with grace,
But slips and lands in soft green lace.

A turtle yawns, begins to roam,
His breakfast choice? A munching foam.
The sunlight tickles blades of grass,
While ants parade, a tiny mass.

The dew drops giggle on the stem,
A ladybug steals breakfast gems.
They chat and laugh in sprightly jest,
As if they know they're nature's best.

And soon the day will shake awake,
With creatures wise, and pranks to make.
But now, in stillness, they unite,
In soft green mornings, pure delight.

Deceptive Quiet in the Wild

The woods seem calm, a sly disguise,
But watch the beetles with their eyes.
They're plotting schemes, a heist for sure,
To swipe some crumbs from nature's cure.

A squirrel grins beneath a tree,
With acorns stashed, a jubilee.
He twirls and leaps, quite the rogue,
While birds debate, "Which seed's a vogue?"

The whispers rustle like a joke,
The rabbit's ears alert to poke.
What is that sound? A sneaky mouse?
Or perhaps a cat, launched from the house?

But laughter spills from every nook,
In this wild world, there's much to crook.
In quietude, mischief lies,
With giggles rising to the skies.

Small Wonders of Earth's Embrace

Beneath the shade of shady trees,
A snail in boots moves with such ease.
He glances back, as if to say,
"Who knew the world would move this way?"

Each pebble speaks, a gossip grand,
They tell the tales of this wild land.
Where mushrooms dance, much to their glee,
A party brewed with nature's tea.

Bright colors spill upon the ground,
A hidden dance, so safe, profound.
A wiggly worm, a shy ballet,
He sways and curves, without delay.

So pause and marvel, if you can,
At tiny wonders, part of the plan.
In this grand world, both wild and free,
Life's little quirks are meant to be!

Illuminated Silence in the Grove

A shadow leaps within the shade,
"What's in your pocket?" asks the glade.
A squirrel with dreams of jelly beans,
He scampers off to share his schemes.

A whisper floats, the crickets jest,
In evening's glow, they spin their quest.
A firefly winks, a flirty prank,
While shadows play upon the bank.

When stillness falls, the night takes hold,
With twinkling stars, both shy and bold.
A raccoon peeks with curious eyes,
As if to say "Oh, what a prize!"

So laugh with wonder, dance in air,
In the grove's silence, there's joy to share.
With golden beams and playful moans,
Illumined secrets, nature's tones.

Silken Threads of Dawn's Light

A green carpet spreads wide,
In the wake of the night,
While critters all collide,
In a comical fright.

The sun peeks with a grin,
Waking up the sleepy,
As squirrels start to spin,
Their dance, oh so creepy.

Gentle dew drops glisten,
Upon each tiny blade,
If plants could just listen,
To jokes that were made.

The world starts to twirl,
With laughter and cheer,
In nature's soft whirl,
The silly draws near.

Secrets Held in the Forest Floor

Whispers of the ground play,
As shadows do prance,
With ants in a ballet,
They mimic a dance.

Curly roots are hiding,
What mischief, oh my!
A snail starts gliding,
While birds just pass by.

The earth holds its laughter,
In pockets of shade,
With critters chasing after,
Each prank that they made.

Around every tree,
Lies giggles and grins,
It's fun for the free,
Where the nonsense begins.

The Breath of Ancient Stones

Rocks breathe with a chuckle,
As vines twist their fate,
A turtle's quick shuffle,
With time, oh so late.

Old stones hold some wisdom,
Yet seem rather shy,
While frogs croak with rhythm,
Their jokes fly on by.

A lizard in costume,
With scales not quite right,
Winks at the bloom's room,
In the golden sunlight.

The stillness is merry,
When nature's awake,
With laughter they carry,
Each step that they take.

In the Embrace of Fern and Fog

Fern fronds wave hello,
In a mystical haze,
As fog starts to flow,
In a playful daze.

The shadows are silly,
And tease with their dance,
While critters grow frilly,
In a wardrobe of chance.

Underneath the soft cover,
A gopher does glide,
With laughter to hover,
In the mist, he hides.

A world full of cheer,
In this whimsical plot,
As we tiptoe near,
To a nature-filled lot.

www.ingramcontent.com/pod-product-compliance
Lightning Source LLC
Chambersburg PA
CBHW071814160426
43209CB00003B/86